Pages *A Memoir*

Musings of a 75-Year-Old Woman

by
Lila Greene

Editors:
Dana Greene, Jim Avakian, Rachel Hanson,
Lisa Trank, Jack Greene,

Front cover:
Lila, Central Park - 1943

Back cover photograph:
Dianne Greene

Graphic Artist:
Jim Avakian

Published by:
Wily Creative, LLC
P.O. Box 74
Erie, Colorado 80516

Copyright ©Lila Greene, 2009
All rights reserved

ISBN: 978-0-615-27527-7

Some of these "Pages" were previously published by
Lila Greene under the title "Gravity" ©2007

No part of this book may be reproduced or transmitted in any form or by any means, electronic or mechanical, including photocopying, recording, or by any information storage and retrieval system, without permission in writing from the copyright owner, except by a reviewer who wishes to quote brief passages in connection with a review in a magazine or newspaper.

My dear readers,

I've asked why am I still here?

So many have left

Most profoundly my soul mate Mel

These are the words of a 75 year old, lucky woman

This book is unique in the fact

that it is lovingly created

with so much encouragement

from all my children

the ones they married

and my grandchildren

With love

and thanks forever

to all the kind

wonderful people

in my life.

This book is dedicated with my love to my children and the ones they married, and my Grandchildren, the precious gifts of my life.

This memoir is for my Mel, my friend, my husband.

To introduce the people within my book:

My Precious Family

In 1953, I met my beloved husband Mel (my Cary Grant)
He was a singer at the Grossinger Hotel in the Catskill Mountains
I was a reservation clerk "working out" to become a comedian
That was an exquisite time
We married
I loved my husband and our children
with a love so grand
It filled my heart with a joy
I had never known

Our Children:

Jack, Dana, Russell, Debra Lisa and Robert married;

Lisa, Jim, Dianne, David, and Stacey

Our Grandchildren:

Georgia, Will, Mila, Maedee, Julea, Ben, Meggie, and Stella

My Childhood Family:

My sister, my three brothers. My Grandma Dora, my Grandpa Harry (they raised us).

My father

My Mother died when I was three. I cannot remember ever seeing her face. Her name was Rose.

We lost dearest Dad on a Sunday, March 26, 2005.

He was still singing with Deb that very last day.

Table of Contents

Musings of a 75 year-old woman	11
Those were the days	41
My beloved children and grandchildren	55
How to survive once you realize you are not the Estee Lauder girl anymore	99
My absurd fear of spiders	133
The precious dogs we were given to love	147
The seasons that I missed the 50 years I lived in Miami Beach and California & My love affair with the moon	169
My beloved husband Mel	199

Musings of a 75-year-old woman

Can you ever think normally without cigarettes?

If you smoked for 50 years?

Even if you don't want to return to smoking?

Tonight I was in bed reading a newspaper

when I saw a jar of cream next to my bed

I should rub my poor little dry feet

with that cream I thought

Because I don't smoke

I picked up the jar of cream and

turned it in a way that it spilled all over me

and my pajamas

This is not foot cream I thought

This is pain cream

And the menthol

Maybe it's good for my cough

No this is something that doesn't happen

to a person who smokes

This menthol, it will not go away

Oh my poor feet!

The case of vanity and gravity

Year 73

Without liposuction

My body has fallen

It started with the eyes

That part of the face has moved to the cheeks

The cheeks to the neck

The shoulders to the waist

And then the falling thighs

My children think that never exercising

Has created my fallen look

My daughter brought me to the gym

And gave me a gift of a personal trainer

I thought this was someone who you did exercise with

I was wrong

This person runs around the gym with you

showing you how to use the equipment

I did a couple of things impressively

But mostly it was a bunch of people

Showing off their gorgeous bodies

She measured my body fat

That I insisted was just my falling body

"Oh no no," she said

In the dressing room, a woman straight out of Playboy

Was taking her time getting dressed

I could not stop staring at her beauty

Swimming, I thought, that's the only way

I just bought a bathing suit from neck to toe

Am I the only one who needs this?

Let me know

Wise Woman Lila

I had to be wise

To survive

An abusive childhood

An abusive father

An abusive stepmother

Left alone in a hotel in Manhattan

At 11 years old

For weeks at a time

Not even knowing there was dirt on my elbows

And people were whispering about me

Without clothes

With just rags to wear

And not allowed to ask

"Do I have a mother?"

My sister was my older sister

Though only one year older

I looked to her for care

She gave me a picture of a beautiful woman

"This is our Mother Rose," she said

When my father married our stepmother

We were told to pretend she was our real mother

I had three brothers

I had to hide the picture of our beautiful Mother

My father never told her he had five children

She never stopped screaming at us

And I went to school

Got a job as a baby-sitter 30 hours a week

They loved me

Their two babies were safe with me

The mother's name was Harriet

She baked a yellow cake that I more than loved

My sneakers smelled and

When I would sleep over

I would hide my shoes on the outside of the window sill

We were living in a mansion in Kew Gardens

I was growing up to be a very Wise Woman

Reflections of a burned out housewife

When I was a young mother of five

my husband worked as an Entertainment Director

at a large hotel in Miami Beach

Every night he would dress for his 17 course dinner

And as soon as his car drove away we would

head out to the newly created McDonalds or Burger King

In those days Burger King had "Yumbo" sandwiches

These were ham and cheese tightly steamed together

This made the selection more complicated

Would it be a Whopper, a Fish Fillet or Yumbo?

All of which we insisted

they cut in half

Life was so simple then

Each of my five children received one dollar

Each would order for her or himself

Lots of times my sons and daughters

and sons and daughters-in-law

Asked how I did it —

This was certainly one of the answers

Eating alone

I so wish I were not a judgmental person

then I would not criticize another

I was alone most of my youth

There was a particular alone time in a hotel in NYC

I had 50 cents for my meals

This was like $5.00 or more today

I went to Bickford's, a restaurant known for

Chocolate Cream Pie

Sometimes I went to the Automat

known to me for their salisbury steak,

mashed potatoes and creamed spinach

I loved these meals, though I was always alone

I learned to eat alone

I liked eating alone

I can't believe some people make such a fuss about not

waiting for them to begin eating

Which person then is judgmental?

Pretend cleanliness in restaurants

Always having been obsessive

about food being kept safe at home

I'm always surprised

at idiocy in restaurants

Subway for example, uses disposable gloves

This is a nice touch

Sometimes I get the feeling that the gloves are meant to

protect them from what they are doing for us

They have the gloves on and realize they are out of something

thus using the gloves to open this massive door

They then return to the scene of the sandwich making

and continue with the same gloves that have gone

who knows where

Then they sneeze, protecting my food

with their gloved hands

I want to leave and forget the whole thing

I go to a bagel shop

Innovatively they only need one glove to make a sandwich

"Why only one glove?" I ask

as I see her ungloved hand touching my bagel

She shrugs her shoulders, "That's the rule," she says

The only way to eat out is if they do the preparation

behind closed doors

And I try not to think about what they are doing without

gloves!

Stay with your hash-browns

Just had breakfast with Jim, Bob, and Stacey

Jim and I made a pact not to order hash browns

We all had cereal, except Stacey

She had eggs (the whites) bacon (turkey)

And hash browns

"I'm eating for two but I'm not going to eat the

hash browns," she proclaimed!

I ate half my oatmeal with the four blueberries Bob gave me

Stacey never ate the hash browns

Bob kept hugging her

I grabbed and ate a hash brown

And luckily the busboy grabbed the plate

And I left

Still thinking did she order those just to torture Jim and me?

Paranoia is a good thing!

You ask, do I spend the whole day at thrift stores?

You want to know how I entertain myself now

when I'm not in the thrift stores?

Well I watch television and

I study peoples face lifts and Botox shots

I keep asking myself

"Do they look good?"

How do they deal with all that pain?

Sometimes I have trouble even looking at these people

I can't even focus on what they are saying

They look so strange

It's hard to look in their eyes

Their eyes are always too wide open

It is creepy watching them

Today I was watching a movie

And I thought they cast the mother in the part because she

looked so Blanche Dubois

Botoxed

Or did they think she looked good?

I think I have more fun in the thrift stores

Duvet support group

I have Duvet Duvet Disorder

Some people and authorities think

this is a bad thing

like Attention Deficit Disorder

But this is a good disorder

Not if your work however, is such

that you are supposed to fold things

hang things up

and put things away

After 2 hours with a Dell tech

I could not stop itching

Because of David McCloskey's genius

I just got my word processor back and saved $300.00

Once life was difficult without an icemaker

Now I am lost without Microsoft Word

How absurd

Lucky Grandma

Sometimes I wonder

How did I find the courage to ice skate?

Once you lose that positive thought

the one that, at 19, believed that was possible

it is no longer possible!

When you put on a necklace

as long as you believe you can clasp these two parts together—

without looking

you can do it!

Today I walked into my bathtub to take a shower

I started sliding all over the bathtub

I somehow miraculously

regained my balance

I stood still in gratitude

and then I saw a whole bottle of shampoo

that was covering the bottom of the bathtub

Boy, am I lucky that I was once a skater!

I just watched my eighth grandchild Stella learn to walk

This is one of the hardest things we all learn to do –

Like a baby bird flying away from the nest

There is the constant praise and joy coming from the parents

for the child and the baby birds

So many years we go up and down steps without a look

It's so natural, we have done it for so long

I was very comfortable pushing a grocery wagon around

But when you start to bring your grocery wagon into the

bathroom and the sandbox

people start to stare

My children suggested a walker

Oh no, please no

I had a shower bench for a week and it was so ugly

It had to go, and it went

These accessories are so medical looking and so associated

with illness and old age

This is not possible

When did I get old?

I want to be the boss of myself again

Maybe there should be a Jr. Sr. Citizen first, so you know

something else is coming

I have decided to get a walker and fill it with flowers –

daisies –

and bring all my grandchildren with me to sing

"Who will Buy Our Beautiful Flowers?"

No one will know that I need a walker – it isn't a walker

It's a flower cart with an Old Woman

and eight talented children singing

Their Mamas and the Papas won't let me do that

Once I was the boss of everything

And my husband would say

running down the stairs

"Listen to Mother"

And they would

Who will buy my beautiful daisies?

One more responsibility:

It is week two of real winter in Colorado
and I've already lost one and a half pair of gloves
I suggest a tree in the center of Boulder
for lost and found gloves and mittens

What to do if you lose your keys, cell phone or glasses

And you have no spare available?
If you are driving with your glasses on and then think
"Where is my cell phone?"
first realize that this is a good thing
because you have your glasses on
and you can see
Resist cursing
Do not start looking everywhere while you are driving
Do not think someone is already calling Bangladesh
with your phone
Think, "This is no big deal
I'm going to find it"
Don't punish yourself
Think "I am a good person without a cell phone
And I can see!"
That's got to be more important

Yesterday I watched two guys looking for keys to one U-Haul vehicle

They were so kind and polite to each other

The vehicle was late for its return and the place

would be closing in twenty minutes

I watched them walk from room to room calmly

Looking everywhere

And then they were back still looking everywhere

I tried not to say anything

but I couldn't stop myself

from thinking

How about driving to U-Haul for a duplicate key?

They came around again

I thought of my husband when he lost his keys

wildly delving into everything

putting the entire house in disarray

"Mel, look on the top. Why do you think they got lost in the

bottom of drawers?"

My son-in-law Jimmy has a theory about this craziness

He thinks there is a jokester (invisible)

that hides them from us

The person who loses the keys

is responsible for finding them

and feeling like a fool

until the jokester puts them back

(giggling to himself)

and we scream with glee "I have them!"

This is stress, and if they are your keys it is your stress!

This is never going to happen again

I always say to myself

(About my cell-phone and glasses also)

But it does

When my husband gets sick he reminds me of Frankenstein

He talks and walks like Frankenstein

I don't know if Frankenstein had as many complaints

But they have the same walk and talk

Close to death

Or life

When he cries out "Jell-O"

Actually I don't know if Frankenstein

had such a broad vocabulary

Thousands of tissues

I don't want to sleep with Frankenstein

The doctor's patient

His face turned into that of a beautiful boy

And he smiled as he sang with his 76 year old patient

A song he used to sing with his father

The patient said he couldn't sing anymore

And yet he did with the kind doctor

who kept smiling like a boy as his patient sang

the whole song loud and passionately

I was surprised they didn't embrace

My life experience

I used to think it would be a good idea

to marry a plumber

In 2005 I realize it would be helpful

to have someone in your family work

for United's baggage department

I'm so sorry Ellen Barkin

What a rude husband you had

What a weird deal you cut

Married to someone who could order you to

pack up and leave

and guard you while you pack so that only

15 million dollars worth of jewelry goes with you

That's outrageous

It's a good thing you had that clause that you get

20 million dollars also

I don't think you are crying

I think you're laughing

You might want to make a film about your hard life

Try not to lie or you might have to give refunds

No, I am not jealous

Just annoyed

You can't make everyone happy

When the West Nile Mosquito

took over Colorado two years ago

I decided to decorate my patio with bird houses

instead of flowers

eliminating the water that was home to the mosquito

I loved the idea of birds chirping and flying around my patio

My neighbor downstairs complained

The mess was unbearable

Well, I had to get rid of the bird food

and the chirping left

The birdhouses remained as a decorative touch

I noticed wasps flying into the birdhouses

I summoned my courage and peaked inside

There were wasp nests in each birdhouse

Very artistic I thought

I was raising wasps

Was this a brilliant invention?

Was this a way to keep wasps out of my house?

Is it cruelty that I trapped the wasps

from all over Longmont?

I thought of carefully placing each birdhouse

in a plastic bag and

throwing them away

I then thought that was too scary

I'm moving tomorrow

I think I'll call Orkin

Do you think wasps sting birds also?

Attention Mr. Milne

Disney has bumped off Owl

Yes, he was a bit of a bore

but wasn't that an important part of the story?

Wonder if they did a study with one year olds

If they ask me

Piglet is my favorite…maybe Roo…

Absolutely Winnie…sometimes there is too much Tigger…

I remember when someone decided to change

Sondheim's lyrics to "Send In The Clowns"

He is still here to protect himself

Sorry Mr. Milne, you deserve better!

Although it is hard to admit

my brain

is sometimes an inch behind the command

I can feel the annoyance of some

as they speak for me

Of course if your arteries are blocked

it takes longer for directives to get to the brain

I am enjoying the slower pace

I think I am

I had to be so fast for so long

I wanted to say thank you

for so much that you have done

So before I forget

Thank you!

Now A.D. Disorder is everywhere you look or listen

There is this happy enraptured couple

that can't take their eyes off each other

like Judy Garland and Mickey Rooney

looked at each other when they were 16

When suddenly the ceiling falls down

or 12 surprise guests arrive

"No problem", the voice over confidently says

"When the time is right 'he' will be ready"

Now I'm saying "the greatest generation"

we know nothing

Hardly any people had plastic or wax faces

like Joan Rivers

I was watching "Days of Our Lives"

Everyone was gorgeous

No one has lines –

I'm talking not one line

Barbara Walters has not one line

I'm sure I will get a major role

when they need a person with a lined face

There will be no competition –

This is a technical story about bras

Idiotic

they close in the back

They have held a myriad of problems my whole life

and then the final blow

the sag

This is not at all a humorous piece

rather a very sad not talked about problem

I looked it up in an Anatomy Book

A woman at 75

with flat long breasts

The first feeling is despair

The second feeling is chafing

I cannot bear to have another unsuccessful fitting

I need a bra to sleep in and to live in

I am past "post menopausal"

but surprises still abound

Please Olga or Bali

Absolutely not Victoria's Secret

Definitely say no to the back clasp

When you are 75

you can't stretch that far

Those were the days

Who will take care of us?

We didn't want anyone to know where we lived

When there was an air-raid drill at school

we did not go home

We went somewhere else

I don't know where we went

I followed my sister Connie

We were very sad in Coney Island

except for going on the merry-go-round

always trying to catch the brass ring

Once I did –

If you gave it back you would get a free ride

I wish I had never given it back

It would have been better to still have the brass ring

Grandma was very old and my brother Kenny

would steal a Chunky from the candy store

It was a penny candy

and Grandma would chase him around the yard

with a butcher knife

We were still all under five and would stare at her

with our mouths

open in fear

Every once in a while I could smell a cigar

and that would mean my father was home

For a prize he would give me the cigar band

I would wear it like a ring

I had three brothers, a sister

a grandmother, an aunt, and an uncle

a grandfather, and a father

I was missing a mother

but I didn't know that anymore

Aunt Matilda was married to Uncle Mike

He limped, played piano, and screamed at her all the time

"Muttie!" he would yell

and she brought him tea in a tall jar

We spent a lot of time with them before Grandma died

Sometimes all five of us would knock on the door

of their apartment

We could hear the radio playing

but they wouldn't answer the door

We would tumble down the steps lonely, hungry and sad

All the world was very poor then

especially me

with no memory of my Mother

My sister says I never stopped crying

My older brother Herbie said I kept asking him

"Who will take care of us?"

And then one night Grandma told me to sleep with her

I don't remember anything except

that Grandma died that night

I could smell my father's cigar

All five of us were sitting on milk crates

There were sheets covering the pictures, the mirrors

and I don't know what else

"Kenny, where's Grandma?"

He pointed to the sky

I knew what that meant

Uncle Mike arrived

He screamed at us

"Herbie, who will take care of us?" I asked again

I could smell the cigar

and I remember screaming as my father told me

I would stay with Uncle Mike and Aunt Matilda

Nothing could be worse, and yet

that was where I stayed

They were not thrilled with their prize either

Connie would go to Uncle Eddie

and the three boys were put in boarding school

We were 13, 12, 11, 10 and 9...

A few months later my Uncle Mike

told my father to come and get me

I hadn't the slightest idea of how to add

and had innocently erased an "F"

on my test paper and changed it

very obviously to an "A"

My father lived alone in the Capital Hotel

in New York City near the Paramount Theatre

He was a gambler and one that went to bookies sometimes

and to the track with the elite

like Elizabeth Arden, at least that was what he said

There were scary calls for J.M., which was his code name

I was coached on how to lie to them

No, I did not know where he was

This of course was true

A poet from Queens

I never told anyone I came from Coney Island

Emily was my friend

at Forest Hills High School

After school we would light up Pall Malls

and buy hot sweet potatoes from a pushcart

My other friend was Diane

After school we would buy a delicious brownie

at a Jewish bakery before getting on the subway

They were five cents each

This nickel was hard to come by

Everyday she would advance me this nickel

And the next day I would have to give it back

The Orphanage

I was three, my brother Kenny was two

It was bizarre we had the same birthday

October 21st

My brother Arthur was six months old

and people couldn't believe his birthday was October 13th

We were like steps they would say

My sister Connie was a year and a half older than me

and our brother Herbie was one year older than her

It was his job to take care of us

I cannot remember my Mother's face

I don't know how we got to the orphanage

My sister says my father dropped us off

One of the things we did, Connie and me

was to use our left hands to write

This was a bad thing

They would tie our left hand behind our back

so we would be unable to use it

I was crying and so they slapped my back really hard

I cried some more

I wanted to find my sister

My father's dog

When I lived with my father

in the Capital Hotel in New York City

I was eleven years old

My Mother had died when I was three

I was very independent and I was left alone quite a lot

I think in a coma, but awake

My only companion was his dog named Teddy

Everyday Teddy and I would walk to White Castle

Her dinner was a hamburger, and she always gobbled it up

Back to the empty room

and I would count and count and say

"Let's count, Teddy, till Daddy comes home"

When he would come home

he would whistle from the street

We were very high up

I was always scared little Teddy would jump

because she was dancing on the window sill

My father changed his name all the time

to hide from "the bookies"

Once I forgot our name

and while I was being paged by a bellboy calling

I didn't remember my name

My father's wife

I was 12 she was 35

She was lucky to find him

He had five children

He only told her of three

Five was too much

to admit to

After all, even the mother had died

I was glad he found her

She was madly in love with him

They bought a mansion – he was rich

In 3 months it was lost on a horse

She screamed and screamed at us

and we scrubbed the floors and dusted the paneled walls

We were to pretend she was our real Mother

I had a picture of my Mother

This was not my Mama

No matter how he yelled at us

none of us could call her Mother

Today is my Mother's birthday

My own life is now almost over and

though I don't remember my Mother's face

I still get very sad on her birthday

I don't want my children to get sad

when they think of me

I want them to laugh

I am going to change today

and celebrate my Mother's life

Happy Birthday dear Mama

You did good!

My beloved children and grandchildren

Waiting for Jack David

*The pot roast my sweet husband made for us in a hot kitchen
in Miami Beach when I was pregnant and nauseous
with my first baby*

This was 1956, way before women showed off

their bellies and bodies

and men and everyone came into the delivery room

and watched the birthing

I was "alone" in the labor room

staring at the wall and the clock

We wore maternity clothes that were basic and ugly

and we shyly looked at our bellies

We did not know if we would have a boy or a girl

My sweet dear husband had the idea that dinner was dinner

and nausea was not a reason for not preparing it

This meant pancakes were not dinner nor were eggs

These were definitely breakfast foods

And so he shopped and cooked and made a pot roast

I remember how proud he was and how delicious that tasted

It was of course comfort food, even before we found out

we needed comfort foods

He was quite a meticulous person

and so there were potatoes cut in exact

quarters and beautifully sliced carrots and onions

and warm tomato gravy

Never will forget how much I loved him

and how much he loved us…his baby

hidden under the blouse

in me

June 21, 2005

Hello my son

You are 48 today at 5:30 p.m.

Once you were my little baby

I thought I couldn't love more

Once you were my little boy

I thought I couldn't love more

And now how appropriate to have shared

what we have shared

Happy Birthday JD Greene

I love you more,

Mom

My darling daughter Day

You could hardly breathe when you saw Aretha

You sat alone in a dark cloaked coat

when you saw "Phantom" on Broadway

I have been jumping with joy since your

wonderful extraordinary tulips in a box

were hand delivered into my arms as were you

a wonderful divine

almost half a century ago

You are such a generous being and beautiful soul

Everyday I wake up to see the beauty of you within my

joyous tulips that arrived the day before Valentine's Day

I am kissing my tulips and I hope you know

how wonderful you are!

Thank you for more than any mother could pray for

I adore you,

Ma

Hello my darling Russ

You are truly an angel man

But first you were an angel boy

A wonderful gift to love more and more

With every day that runs away from us

You have changed the world with your music

and your brilliant mind

How wonderful for all of us that you have touched

I wish you joy and all that you wish for yourself

You are my Angel Boy and life is very sweet because of you

I will love you eternally

and my heart will be filled with the joy of being loved by you

The world is a sweeter and better place because of you

Happy 47th Birthday Russell Scott Greene

Forever,

Ma

And she never stopped smiling

When our Debra Lisa was born

We all whispered she is the most beautiful baby

in the nursery and she was!

It wasn't easy for Deb to have any time alone with Mama

Because her brother Russ, 3 years older,

was in the hospital at the same time

I thought this could work…as I always think

everything can work

They told me Russ would sleep all day…

a three-year-old boy with energy

What did they know!

When we went home, Jack and Dana

could not wait to play with our new "Dolly"

Russ was already recovered from his surgery

and ready for mischief

I was begging for quiet just to rest with my baby and me

And so Dad took all three out for sundaes

and the quiet came at last

That time will always remain in my heart

There she was my miracle, and she was smiling a smile

And a smile in her beautiful green eyes

Dearest Debra Lisa

HAPPY BIRTHDAY and many more!

I remember my son Robert in an afro bringing me

a delicious cup of soup
in a restaurant a long time ago
Always the mother feeling taking over
thinking of rushing up to you
and hugging and kissing you
although I know you would not have yelled at me
I can still imagine a look of disdain
that would have appeared on your face
Dad and me nourished by you, our Bob
And the whole world was in love with you
You were "easy" and Dad tucked his napkin in
and glowed with pride over your industrious self
You are a very special man, brother, husband, father
and son
Dad, you know how shy he was
never stopped raving about you
I think he's got Pavarotti's attention and singing
"My Boy Bobbo"
You are our bonus
and I say Bravo, too!

Once upon a time there was a man who proclaimed;

I'm never getting married

Once upon a time there was a girl

while carrying food to her customers saw him

their eyes met

He shyly from the corner of his eye as he prepared oysters

This was the beginning of the breakdown of his marital plans

Lisa is beautiful – unbelievably blue eyes

A skin made of porcelain

Lisa is smart

He went to New York

So did Lisa

They were always together after that

They came back to Boulder

and made a life

They got their Masters' degrees at Naropa

and then they married

A magnificent wedding high in the mountains

where the wind would practically

blow down the chupa

A reception at the Boulder Museum on 13th Street

How creative and strong she is

Mila Donne Rose was born

While still nursing Mila

two babies arrived

Twins of course

Two girls

Maedee and Julea

The challenge was gigantic

Lisa never compromised her excellence in caring

So much has happened since Lisa at 37

arrived in Boulder

Yes, she's a little bit older

Yes, she's married her man Jack

They are madly in love

They have three amazing daughters

Boulder has opened its arms to a woman

who is talented

loving

beloved

and FIFTY today

Happy Birthday dear Lisa

We can't wait to play!

My dear beloved Jimmy
May 15th 2008

So much history

I am honored to be your mother-in-law

I think we should get you a Super-Jim outfit

When you fixed the piano on the road the last time

I thought, "How does he do it?"

And I knew it was a unique genius and strength

because I'm sure it wasn't one of the "Vows"

With a deep love and respect

I join the family in wishing you happiness

on your 54th Birthday

Forever,

Lila

Where do the birds go when it snows?

For My Precious Daughter-in-Law Dianne on her
50th Birthday, whose grace and charm have always
reminded me of a sweet bird

Hundreds of birds flew onto my beautiful pine tree just now

And as they landed, lots of snow fell

from the tree to the ground

And as I stood in awe

They were on their way again

Where are they going?

One bird was taking her time

I stood close to the sliding door and said softly

"You better hurry – Where will you go in the snow?"

She chirped, "This is my job – I'm making sure

the family is all here

We are going to California

We have to be there before the winter Solstice

We'll be back in March"

And she flew away

never mentioning her 50th birthday

December 14th, 2007

Many reasons I love David McCloskey

My precious Debra loves him

Will, Benny and Meggie adore him

He lets everyone call him Charlie

He was exceedingly kind to dear Dad

He said nothing when I broke the dishwasher

And nothing when I broke the insert to his microwave

His focus is awesome

He started SuperStructs in a loft in his house

with an outrageous amount of interruptions

He loves our family

We all love him

He is strong

He is kind

He is very polite

He loves his family

He didn't complain when Rocky bit him in his own house

He is an amazing Father

He loves our Debra Lisa

and darling Will, dear Ben and precious Meggie Meg Meg

He is a great tech

and did not complain when I could not figure out

how to turn the T.V. off

You are a great guy Charlie McCloskey

and I wish you a 45th Birthday filled with joy and love and

happiness!

The MIL

Stacey is my third daughter-in-law

She is beautiful

and Bob is madly in love with her

Many years ago before they were married

Bob had emergency surgery

It was a scary life-threatening situation

I think this was before they were living together

I flew in from Colorado (on a plane of course)

We could not find Stacey

I said I would stay overnight

to comfort him

The next thing you know Stacey arrived

There she was looking like the front cover of Cosmopolitan

There I stood confronted with the thought

that I was out of a job

I asked myself who would he rather have stay with him

His mother or his breathtakingly stunning girlfriend Stacey?

She of course was massaging his feet

I went home with Dana and Jim

One of the most beautiful things to be

Is a Grandma

The second carousel ride of my life

To love and be loved

On the next level of love

The ride

On the way to the sky

How lucky am I

Grandma Lila

Georgia calls me Grammy

And I think I'm in a movie

I am dazzled

And my heart jumps with joy

Grandma, it is the role of a lifetime!

My darling granddaughter Mila
on the occasion of your 9th birthday

You have always been such an endearing human being to me

from the day that you were born

and Grandpa Mel held you in his arms and cried with joy

We were lucky to be able to spend a lot of time with you then

I was able to walk around your apartment in Boulder

pushing your stroller

and you would sing to me

and all the people that were walking by

You were and are so adorable

So beautiful

You are our 3rd grandchild

Your dedication to your violin

and to all that you touch is inspiring to me

and to Grandpa Mel

Your adoration of your two sisters

and how you waited for them to be born

with such love

You called them your angels

Your love and respect for your Mama and Papa

makes you so special

We will always love you

and always be cheering for you

and your happiness

You are beloved by us

Happiest Birthday Lovely Mila Donne Rose

Always my heart,

Grandma Lila

My amazing grandson Will

When you were very little and you started to draw

I was so excited for your talent

When you started to write those poems I was amazed

When you began to read all your chapter books

I could hardly believe it

You are an ARTIST and a SCHOLAR

You are a caring sensitive person

Love always,

Grandma Lila

Superstar status

When I was a young mother

my kids enjoyed

scaring me

Now they are loving me with such a love

I cannot find the words to say how happy they make me

It's like dancing

It's like singing

They are enchanting

Their children scream

"It's Grandma! It's Grandma! It's Grandma!"

I am Arthur, I am Barney, I am Big Bird

I am their Grandma

And that makes Me

a celebrity!

I love their voices

and the new voice they come with

I love their happiness

I love watching my children love them

I love their energy

I love the Aunties and Uncles adoring them

I love how they love me

Another gift of life

These precious innocent souls

What do I feel?

I feel my heart explode

Benny called today

First the Mama got on the phone

"There's a cowboy here that wants to talk to you"

"Grandma, I'm wearing my boots"

"Oh Ben, that's wonderful"

"Grandma, I'm wearing my boots"

"Oh Ben, I love you and miss you so much"

"Grandma I'm wearing my boots

You want to talk to Mama?"

Have you ever loved a child?

Can you hear my heart aching?

I am a Grandmother now

And two of my grandbabies "afterbirths"

are in my freezer

waiting to be planted

Being a grandmother is all I dreamed it would be –

Just a little more delicious than being a Mama

if that is at all possible

It's all a rerun

except you have the moment

to survey their inner souls

When they say "Grandma"

a new joy runs all around my heart

When they get sick, an old pain confronts me again

I love to watch them "watch"

Life is beautiful indeed

On being a Grandma

This role comes with so many glorious recommendations

I never knew what to expect

Could I believe that we had a family?

And that they were real

And they would have children

And they would be real

When I saw Teresa Heinz

touch her hand to her heart

as her son spoke for his step-father, John Kerry

I knew exactly what she was feeling

My body has always been an explosive of love

for my children

And now another gift has fallen upon me:

My Grandchildren

"Here, Grandma I made this for you"

Oh Will, how happy my heart feels from your love

Your commitment

With each day I love you more

than the day before

And then there's Ben

One minute with a binky a bottie and a blankie

and only a heart for Mama or Papa

And then he turns into

Bennie and a multitude of superheroes

He's all dressed as Buzz Lightyear at 6 A.M.

And this gorgeous 2 year old climbs up the steps

and declares, "To Infinity and Beyond!"

Love Sick

When a child is sick your whole world is gone

My little Grandson Ben is sick today

and I can't stand it

Suddenly Buzz Lightyear is gone also

The laughter has flown

Oh please, please make him better again

Dear Ben, I love you so

Mixed up

My adrenalin is mixed up

When I hear Ben scream

I react as if there is a lion in the room

David is calm "He's alright," he says

Kind of chuckling at my mixed up adrenaline

and very superior in his calmness

There is also a baby sitter

calmly sipping water on the floor next to baby Megan

Oh the glass, the glass, I think

I must look into the Sr. Citizen's activities today

Sweet Georgia Malane is 11

I remember putting her in her carriage

She was a tiny little gem

I was scared and so I tried to move very slowly

She was my first grandchild

and I didn't know what I was feeling

Something extraordinary

A beautiful baby girl born out of the love

of Dianne and Russell

She was always so charming

It is amazing how charming she is

Her spirit is always flying and taking me with her

and she's taught me what a granddaughter is

Right out of a magical book there is that joyous smile

That jolt of love

When I was having trouble climbing the steps

there she was

carefully assisting me

Slowly, as I once put her in her carriage 11 years ago

she helped me up the steps

Oh Georgia, you are wonderful indeed

Georgia, you are so dear to me

I love you with a love that is like a tight moment of string

You are tied to my heart forever

Happy Birthday sweet Georgia you precious gift

and September 14th

shall always be engraved in Gold

Love you eternally,

Grandma Lila

My Bennie Boy just called me on the phone

"I'm better Grandma, stop worrying

Buzz Lightyear is back!"

Loving and living

A great risk

If you think about it

It's so fragile

Well I'm moving soon

All is gone from my freezer

except for a box of banana popsicles

a half a loaf of spelt bread

and a cake tin containing the "placentas"'

of Maedee and Julea

Life is fragile, indeed!

The old drama queen and our twin girls, Maedee & Julea

I used to say, "And life goes on…and this is a good thing"

First there has to be torture

I finally found a radio station and the ability to

change the stations

so I could spend my time in the car listening to the love songs

of the 40's

and know that my dear husband

was as good as any of them

I could sing all the lyrics and dream

He is gone and it is so final

The songs that he sang are deeper in my heart

Me the most prompt person I ever knew

Mel always late…always rushing

Always primping, always dapper, always handsome

I am now arriving at Maedee and Juleas' 6th birthday party

I am late

The twins leave their guests and run to my car

There is no Grandpa in sight

They love me and I adore them

Their beautiful "big" sister Mila is right behind them protecting them

Life goes on, and that's a good thing

The radio is off, but I still can hear him singing

"I've Got You Under My Skin"

The kids stare at me, as I respond with the next line

"I've got you deep in the heart of me

So deep in my heart, you're really a part of me"

That male voice, I sure do miss it

I'm at the joyous party

We enter together

Happy Birthday Maedee and Julea

And many, many more!

Waiting for Meggie

It is August 21

Meg is 3 days late

I know what her middle name is

It is Alise

Meggie Meg Meg

arrived on August 21

Could it be – would there be another Deb?

Will and Benny knew that they would have a sister!

I was the assistant to the Papa babysitter

when Deb became a Weight Watcher lecturer

My beautiful little Maggie and I became so close

It was extraordinary to watch her keeping up with the boys

To see that breathtaking smile again

The sparkling blue eyes

Meg is going to Kindergarten in September

My seventh grandchild

just outgrew the Princess stage

and is in love with Hannah Montana

What a privilege to watch her grow!

Benny goes to school

Oh Ben

Beautiful sweet funny courageous Ben goes to school

He told me "Grandma it's scary"

I try not to cry

and I am reminded

of Deb in her yellow dress going to kindergarten

while Bob in Dad's tie stood by with Jack, Dana, and Russ

and smiled

My heart goes with you dear Benny

Wish we could have a Slurpee together later

Let's go see Herbie at the movies

A trip to the movies with Will and Ben

is a big deal money-wise

Tickets – one senior, two children

$20.00

Two sodas

$7.00

Two small popcorns

$7.00

Out of money?

Don't worry, they like Visa

Ben wants to know where Mama is

He is leaving

Will isn't

Oh this is more than a $30.00 investment

And this is a high point in the movie for Will

"O.K. Ben, let's sit in the aisle on the steps

and wait for Mama"

We sit in the aisle, me watching Will, Ben thinking it over

"Where's Mama?" he persists

"Will, come on let's go get some candy"

We're back at the crooked candy counter

The candy is $3.50 each

After my first winning statement

That they listened to "no chocolate"

(Somebody has to be the boss)

We returned to our seats

Reserved with spilled popcorn and stashed sodas

Now the tab was up to almost $40.00 plus cavities

I forgot to tell you Deb gave me $30.00 dollars

I remembered going to the movies alone

With a treasured dime my Grandfather had given me

At least sixty years ago

What did I get for my dime at the movies?

We weren't allowed to buy anything at the candy counter

The movies started with horse races

You got a number with your ticket purchase

If your horse came in you would get a prize

There was a lot of screaming during the race

I remember winning once

The prize was copper sheets and a hammer

To design things

Mostly I loved the Shirley Temple movies

They said they needed a mop to handle my tears

I didn't like the cartoons at all

It was a whole day at the movies

That's what you got for a dime

And that dime was not easy to come by!

I am sitting in the biggest chaos

I have ever created

Christmas Chanukah and birthday presents all over my bed

I am overwhelmed by my habits

I pray for Christina, Deb or Russ to come save me

And so I take a break and read a few folk tales

And think this book would be good for Georgia

But some of this collection is really scary

Maybe I should save it

Read it to Georgia, Will and Mila

As the traveling Grandma

Grandpa walks in and out very quickly

Now I say here is a birthday present for Lisa

But I'd really like to read it first

But Jack would like it more

Di's gift is in the mail

There are perfect presents for almost everyone

Lavender for Day

A scarf and sleeveless sweater for Deb

Legos for Will

Buzz Lightyear for Ben

What do I have for the men?

I'm getting such a headache

And finally I remember

A bib for our Meg

Who could forget Maedee and Julea

They told me their pantyhose were broken

Sometimes I wish I was a Virgo

Stella, my beautiful wonderful caboose Grandchild

We were all in the hospital

with Jack on the phone

waiting anxiously for the arrival of

our Stella Matil

It was going to be a C-Section after all

Stacey's parents were there, too

We were a crowd waiting for our Rock Star to be born

and when they screamed to us all was well

we cheered and the nurses were rolling their eyes at us

We were a large group (and a little loud)

Stacey's mother saying, this is my first grandchild

Me saying, this is my eighth grandchild

not realizing, that put me in 2nd place of Grandmothers

to hold our little Stella Matil

Stella has grown up in Venice

She is a real beach baby like her Mama and Papa

Dana and Jim are the Godparents'

and Georgia has another cousin that adores her

However, Stella lives near Georgia

and they are in love with each other

Auntie Dianne and Uncle Russell

make the perfect support system

I miss watching lil' Stella growing –

the Godmother keeps me updated

Little Stelly has (by herself) created a stage (from a suitcase)

and a microphone (from a toy)

She loves to entertain and her parents

Stacey the dancer and Bob the musician

are blown away by her preciousness

Auntie Day and Uncle Jimmy (the Godparents)

are the producers for Stella

Would you believe she already has a saleable CD

I miss her!

This is the up side

There is nothing like the feeling

That you feel when you see your kids

As Parents, as Aunts and Uncles

With the wondrous people they marry

And their hands in yours

Now as big or bigger than yours

And a hug from one

Who has become a woman or man

And will always belong to your heart

To witness that they have a place of their own

And they have learned to get along in the world

And see how industrious they are

and Kind

and Kind

and Kind

Doing the right thing especially if you are a Libra

When your children are about nine years old

You can no longer tell them things like

Not to pick up a whole tomato with a fork

And when you ask your loving family to watch your dog for three months

It is no longer your dog

With all the love that is in my heart

For probably the cutest dog on the planet

I mean all dogs are so beloved and some are beauteous

Some are darn right irresistibly, irrepressibly adorable

Some with popcorn toes

Rock to me is all the dogs we've ever loved

And so I am giving my precious Rock

With all my heart

To the Trank-Greenes

Because I'm a Libra

And I have to do the right thing!

*How to survive
once you realize you are not the
Estee Lauder girl anymore*

My life at almost 72

Mel thought he was having a heart attack

and so we spent the last three days in the emergency room

and the hospital

This is what we call entertainment when you are in

your 70's

It's the vacation mode

Eating like a freshman in college

Macaroni and cheese, potato soup and a side of carbs

Mostly wonderful nurses, but the one you remember

is like Nurse Cratchett in

"One Flew Over The Cuckoo's Nest"

I stayed on a cot, pretty comfortable except for the endless

interruptions to get blood, vitals, etc. from Mel

He did not wake up for any of these searchlight interruptions

Just me....what can I eat...where are the carbs?

You save a lot of steps when you don't smoke anymore

There is a waiting room

There is a lot of waiting in a hospital

I start tearing out recipes out of their magazines…

everyone is looking at me

Suspiciously…baked chicken, pan fried cod…

I now have 25 recipes and then the doctor arrives and says,

"Everything's fine, come see the movie"

I don't tell him I don't understand one thing he's saying

or I'm seeing

Kinda like the way I react looking at

the 3 month old embryo's film

Does anyone care that I really can't see?

"Look at this – a graft that detached itself

No problem. Good, good, good," he continues

Mel, wake up, here come the carbs

Too much Ativan

"Where did you go?" my neighbor asked

"Vacation," I said

Boulder Community Hospital

I think I gained 10 lbs.

It's the carbs you know!

I don't smoke anymore

Everyone has something to say about growing old

No matter how old they are

And there are very strict rules about it

If you are 3 like my grandson Ben

And you're going to be 4 tomorrow

today you are still 3 – period

If you are entering your 30's, beauty has already departed

40, definitely you're out of work

50, they still have makeup ideas

60 is really high maintenance, according to Nora Ephron

When will someone speak up for 70?

I am going to be 74 tomorrow

Talk about high maintenance

It happens so fast

There is no time to ponder

I'm going to be 74 tomorrow, but today

I'm still 73 like my Bennie

Gonzo – Take me along stain remover

Some people are stain resistant

I attract stains

The latest seems to be stains on dark clothes

How does a black T-shirt get stains?

Nothing got the stains out

Today I found "Gonzo"

It works!

I'm so surprised!

Please pass the mustard

It's Sunday one day before Valentine's Day

I had to go to the chiropractor Friday

Mel took me

It was probably from the spin in the shower on Tuesday

Sciatic nerve

It's happened before

I'm itchy

Mel also has a rash

We have to wash all the linens

We live in a cold climate

There are many layers

Why don't I live in a hotel, in a warm climate

With room service

We have a heating pad filled with beans

Our carousel in the micro-wave has broken

The bag burned and opened in the microwave

without a carousel

The beans are dropping all over my sciatic nerve

I just slipped and only two legs dropped off my coffee table

There is a cut and a need for peroxide

and a band-aid for my elbow

I pass Mel to get the Band-Aid from his bathroom

"What are you doing?" I ask

"Checking my blood pressure," he says

A hotel… we need to move to a hotel

With room service!

Do you remember all six of us painting the house on La Gorce?

Our Bob was four, not quite five —

all the Gemini's birthdays were coming up

only our Deb had a birthday that year

we were all throwing paint around

I remember it was spring because

it was horrendously hot in Miami Beach

and we were all dressed wrong for the cool L.A. night

We all fit in a car with three dogs and the luggage

I was only thirty-six

Dad looked handsome as ever and he was the reason

we moved to L.A.

with reckless abandon

We got the money for our plane trip by selling the piano

We gave the Falcon to the gardener in trade

and we became different than the east coast people

They say "You can't go home again"

Everyone we knew in Miami is still there

The road not taken, needed so much clearing

But look who you all are!

I went to the movies alone today

I wanted to see The Prairie Home Companion

It wasn't very crowded

But almost everyone was a couple

I can't stand sitting next to a stranger

Or someone blocking my view

So I placed my hat on the seat in front on me

And my purse and soda on the seat next to me

Which used to embarrass Dad

But I didn't care, the movie was empty

I thought about seeing Picnic at Radio City Music Hall

With Dad more than 50 years ago

And so many other movies with my hand on his knee

And his hand on my hand

I missed the intimacy of that moment

There were a lot of trailers and then the real movie

Kevin Kline dressed very dapper very 40's

With a hat

He was very Dad

And suddenly I wasn't alone

He had his arm around me

I loved that

We have to do that again

I wish I could see all my friends again

In one room when

Rob Roy's were still in fashion

And smoking was an o.k. thing

Oh, to go back to those days again

Memories of such excitement and

So much love

All squeezed into a lifetime

And so much laughter

And the excitement of playing with a super-star

Gosh that was fun

Miss you, our friends

And mostly I miss you my beloved

Remember?

Dear Nora Ephron,

I hate my neck also! And my shoulders that

sneakily one morning

Landed on my waist

And I wish my complaints were heard before yours

And then I remember some of the surgeries

my friends have been through

And it is easier to put on my makeup in the dark

and shut-up

I was in the emergency room yesterday

A hospital is where they do their best to

make you look ugly

The gowns have not improved in colors or style

for a whole century

They still can't stay closed

This is no accident

They attach many needles and machines

Then they leave you in a room with no food and not the right

TV channels for hours

When you finally find the remote

You learn that a 92-year-old woman is being told that

Her husband's discovery of "Pluto"

Is no longer recognized

Everyone who walks by is staring at your weird outfit

I still hate my neck Nora but I'm going home

This absurd trip probably cost $5,000

I should have had my neck lifted

About sex and the movies

What is my truth?

Only the movies told us what to do

What was romance?

What was a kiss?

What do they know?

A perverted director?

Who told Clark Gable what to do?

And thusly we all followed them

Fruitless

There was a long while lately when all seemed fruitless

And now it is gone and I'm so glad

Where does it come from, that terrible place?

Productive again

Can we survive without many caring?

A writer writes Russ said

I'm here Deb said

I'm here Dana said

Lisa said we're going to empty your garage tonight

Oh it is too cold for you

No it isn't she said

No we can't survive without the caring

A writer writes

Status

The question surprised me

As I was being questioned for an X-ray application

"Marital Status"

"Widow"

"O.K."

(That was the first time I have answered that question with

that word)

I started to cry and she passed a box of tissues

And suddenly she too was crying

When I left for the waiting room

I thought

Why didn't I just say single?!

Why did I have to say, "Widow?"

A man came to lead the way to the X-ray room

A little boy was wandering in the hall

"I think he's lost," I said

The man yelled down the hallway

"Are you lost?"

"Yes!"

"Wait there," and turned

Continuing to take me wherever I was to go

"Oh no," I said,

"Help him, now"

The boy-being a boy, had exited a room where there was

no re-entry

And he was lost

And me, I was a little lost also

Status, Part Two

"Just put your things on the chair and lie down…

Don't worry, the machine will tell you what to do"

He watched me lay down and told me to move further back

I did and he left

Suddenly the bed went all the way under

the X-ray equipment

It was very still

I was alone

Abruptly the machine demanded, "Hold your breath"

I was thinking maybe the machine broke

and I should start breathing

without the machine's permission,

When again the voice said, "Breathe"

This was to happen one more time and then

Someone came and said,

"That's it. You can go now"

And I did

Once we were all so strong and industrious

And suddenly that time is gone

We hardly noticed it go

I don't think we noticed it at all

But when I remember how many dogs have come

And left

I realize a lifetime has passed

There are meds for this and meds for that

We are staying longer on the planet earth

The medicines have disastrous side effects

But here we all still are

Oh for the days when an alka-seltzer could fix anything

Are you claustrophobic?

"Are we talking plane? Elevator?"

"No," the Doctor replies

"MRI. I want to see if you broke your sacrum

and that is the problem"

"Yes! YES! I am mega claustrophobic"

Are they kidding, not an inch of breathing room?

"I'll prescribe 5 mg of Valium 20 minutes before the test"

"Hello, this will only take 20 to 30 minutes

What kind of music do you like with your MRI?"

"Very mellow please"

I lie down and the technician speaks no words except

"Here is the panic button"

I'm in, "Where did you say the panic button is?"

Russell said he writes songs to distract himself

Why are they hammering on this tube

Oh man, how can I hear the mellow music

Just think of when you met Mel and fell in love

I'm smiling just thinking of the moment

each of our five babies arrived

"Can I get a break?" I resist pushing the button

"Rest in between the labor"

This is the nurse at De Paul hospital in Norfolk

while I'm in labor with Dana

"If we stop then we'll have to start at the beginning

It's just 3 more minutes"

I can do this! It's Nemo speaking

The Doctor calls very soon "you have a broken sacrum"

This is good news, I now know MRI's are a good thing,

and I am a brave old lady!

Introspective

It is almost 41 years since

the last of my five babies were born

"She has babies like lollipops my husband would brag"

This totally annoyed me since he had no idea

what he was saying

But now I know

I was very young

as most of us mothers were of that generation

And if there was trouble conceiving, people adopted

And the love was the same

And I didn't think much about it, though people were in

deep pain

Because I had babies like lollipops

But about twenty years ago scientific progress brought another

dimension to

The people, who couldn't have babies like lollipops,

like me

And new names for new processes were casually

thrown around

No one was interested in my ridiculous information

It had now come back to money and percentages

Someone I love very much just had this procedure

If you buy two chances your third chance is free

They only bought one with a twenty percent chance

of having a baby or two babies because of

the age of her eggs

Every part of her body felt pregnant

She was still giving herself shots in

her stomach today as she had done everyday

since the insemination

She bravely went to the Doctor

and a smiling nurse greeted her

This is going to be good news she thought,

just look at her smile

They walked into the private office and sat down

"It is not good news, dear"

Why doesn't she stop smiling?

Lila's tricycle

When I got up and ran through my rolodex of problems

I remembered

And a picture rolled into my mind

My own red tricycle

That a kind man named John gave me yesterday

Rock looked at me

Are we going out for our walk?

Of course Rock!

We both ran downstairs

And there it was in the garage

Good morning red tricycle

And I pulled it out

Rock eyed it suspiciously

But he was with me wherever I would go

Even on top of this big giant thing

I was a little nervous

This was going to work for me

Rock and I would be going over meadows

And laughing and admiring my thin thighs

It was a little difficult steering and stopping

I needed practice

What fun this was going to be

My own red tricycle that

A man named John gave to me

Lila's red tricycle, day 2

An afterthought

I didn't know how to ride a bike

It was not on the agenda during the depression

And the last time I jumped on someone's bike

To show my father I could ride

I was probably twelve

I was headed straight through a trolley

I stopped by turning over the bike

And spraining my ankle

My father told me I was an idiot

And now I am seventy-one and my chance has come again

I just need to tell myself

I can do it!

Rock says, yes you can!

It is so amazing the amount of Klutziness old age has brought upon me

Of course the meds don't help

Do you know that a person could get

Black and blue all over just from baby aspirin?

I was beginning to get used to it, even surprised

when anyone would inquire

about how bruised I am

Well the other night I got up from bed and banged my eye

right into a lamp

My personality is very quick to overlook things

I thought about going to the kitchen and getting some ice

But I didn't

The next morning I awoke with a little bruise around my eye

Why didn't I get the ice?

Things have gotten worse

Now my eye is very swollen and red as if I had been in a boxing match

I noticed cans keep falling on my toes

I'm sure people are staring at me

I just read that they are pulling the Palm Trees from

Beverly Hills and Miami Beach

Not just because the coconuts fall on old

people's heads, but they noticed

other trees give more shade without bruising

When we lived on Miami Beach, we used to eat

the coconuts that fell from our very own tree

We never thought, as the seven of us laughed

while devouring that delicious coconut,

how much shade we were missing

I went to California for the holidays

Five of my arteries are blocked

I can't walk and minutes away from missing my plane

back to Colorado because we forgot to take

my medicines from Dana and Jim's house

My son in law Jim, runs back to get the meds

I'm looking at my watch and not allowed to get into the

reserved wheelchair until

the other wheelchair arrives

Jim will be here in a few minutes

The other person starts screaming that

she's going to miss her plane

She looks more miserable then me because she has oxygen

I'm torn between giving her the wheelchair

and missing my plane

Jim shows up and so does another wheelchair

If you're old

And live in a world where no one has wrinkles but you

A world of constant erectile dysfunction commercials on T.V.

And where what was once your beautiful dimples

fall in a heap on your face

And if your cell phone is missing and you finally find it in the bag with

the raw chicken in the fridge

You think your shrink likes you but only your dog and your grandchildren like you

You're not getting fat, you're getting short

Without botox, hair color, liposuction

Without a computer instructor

You're not the Estee Lauder Girl anymore

Although it is hard to admit

My brain

Is sometime an inch behind the command

I can feel the annoyance of some as they

speak for me

Of course if your arteries are blocked it takes longer for directives to get to the brain

I am enjoying the slower pace

I think I am

I had to be so fast for so long

I wanted to say thank you

For so much that

You have done

So before I forget

Thank you!

Retirement living

I am here by a total accident of fate

Sometimes I think this is not an accident

While I am thinking about this

it's Thursday already

Once long ago when I still had skin without creases

I went on a cruise with my husband to Jamaica

Everyday we woke up it was still Tuesday

Now time is just spinning away

and I realize how little I know

50 was a big surprise

I thought I was so smart, I wasn't

It was an hour later that I was 75 and

the beauty faded and fortunately

I was enveloped with love

I loved so many people

and I wanted to hug almost everybody

I remember My Mel saying

"Please don't kiss everybody,

then they expect me to kiss them also"

I never thought that you wouldn't be here

Right now I would love to kiss and hug you

I wouldn't let go

Not this time

My absurd fear of spiders

The spiders are having a party in my bathtub

The spiders are having a party in my bathtub

First I spotted one

It looked like a black widow

Then her twin sister

Oh man, I live in Boulder

My kids and friends are all conservationists

I have to take these spiders out to a safe place

I'm so big

They're so little

I'm so old

They're so young

Why am I so scared?

The spider saga continues

No big deal

Look in the tub

Someone from the same group is here

Frozen in fear

From the light

I'm still scared

But experienced and prepared

Grab the mousse

And spray

Can you guys take a break?

It's Saturday

Goodbye dear spiders

I finally locked them out

Since they always were in the bathtub

And with my great detective skills

I finally assumed they were lost

Taking a wrong turn and

Coming out from the drain by accident

Probably on their way to a dance in the pipes

I was depressed from murdering them

And so again I closed the drain

It didn't look too secure so I put 10 wash clothes

on top of the drain

I woke up many times during the night

but never did I see a spider

I thought I heard a dinosaur in the walls

So I had a cup of tea

Maybe it was just Rock breathing

Angels in the bathtub

I am laughing at myself

It's hard to be afraid of spiders

when you're laughing at yourself

I am not a structured person

Not at all

But I now have a regime

I hastily take my shower

All the time thinking of the spiders

I am so glad it's not snowing out because

All this preparedness would not be possible if I was cold

I shut off the water

Release the showerhead

Wait for all the excess water to leave the tub

I close the drain

Place one dry washcloth on it

Place my 20 pound pink angel statue

on top of the closed drain

Carefully leave the shower thinking

You better be more careful

And then congratulate myself on finding a place

for my beautiful angels

in my serene new room

I'm not afraid of spiders

I have control of my environment

There are pink angels (a precious gift from Dana)

Guarding the bathtub

In my new life

In my new room

Again a spider, again a blunder in science

After having not seen a spider for days since

the washcloths and the Angels were blocking the drain

I was about to enter the shower/tub when I saw one

Oh, they have a lotta legs I was thinking

I turned on the shower – he panicked

I started throwing water at him

He started running away

I grabbed the mousse

Goodbye I thought as I kicked him down the drain

with no remorse

Only the thought, "Was he here before I removed the Angels

and the washcloth?"

I am not a scientist

I am a coward

Sherlock Holmes is stymied

Last night I saw a 4 foot...Mosquito

It had quite a bit of nerve

And I knew one of us would not make it through the night

It was flying so fast I grabbed my hairspray

and sprayed it around my whole body

Sure, I knew it was poison

and I watched my victim fly and fly and fly

I didn't see it and assumed it had expired

But then there it was again

I got the mousse and with almost the whole can

got the mosquito

and let him lay upon the wall

Why?

Did I want a spider to get it?

Or was it just a trophy of my new found courage

I woke up and with all my barricades

there was another spider

Angels and washcloths were no defense

I grabbed the mousse

then grabbed the spider

sent it down the drain

And am still obsessing about my fate

I remember getting up every morning

In California for a while and being surprised

That my car had been broken into

In an unsuccessful attempt to steal my radio

So today when I saw what seemed like the exact same spider

I murdered yesterday

I reached for the mousse

Took aim, goodbye

I have bought so much hair product that does not

Help my hair at all

Finally I know what to do with at least a year's supply

Spiders in Erie

A spider just ran across the wall at about 75 miles an hour

I couldn't help but scream out "Deb! Spider!"

With the same urgency that one screams "FIRE!"

Was I crazy? Was I really calling for help?

I was sorry I called her

What a jerk I felt like as I hunted for the speeding spider

With my hair mousse can in my hand ready to fire

"He got away Mom, Goodnight"

Easy for her to say

Although it didn't really seem as if he was looking for me

"Goodnight"

She was back in a second

"Can I borrow that mousse for my hair tomorrow?"

'Piders are good

My granddaughter Mila is 6

"Grandma, 'piders are good, don't be afraid of 'piders"

she said when she was two

And she smiles so big not even thinking

that all her front teeth are missing

Will is seven and very practical and

short of patience with me

"Now look Grandma, you are 15 million times

bigger than that 'pider

You look like a giant next to that 'pider

Grandma, 'piders are good"

And then Luna (his dog) starts barking at a horse on TV

And I turn off the TV and

My sister (in California) hears the barking

on the phone says,

"Oh how funny, another voice to choose a channel"

Live and Let Live

'Piders are good

I'm so sorry but I have to admit

I drowned the spiders

I just couldn't figure out

How to get the jar for their exit and watch them

At the same time

Once they saw me and started running

I had to take action

The song turned on in my head

"Oh the insy-winsy spider went up the water spout –

Down came the mean grandmother and

washed the spiders out"

O.K. now I close the drain so they can't ever come back

Now I have to stand in my own shower water

Because the drain won't open

And I can't tell anyone this story

Even the person who can release the drain

I murdered a spider this morning

I did it with mousse

I feel like a bully

But a creative one

This is my final re: fear of spiders

I am plagued with confusion

First I was sure the spiders were coming up

from the bathtub drain

Still I continued to see spiders in the bathtub

with the drain securely fastened down

with two angels and four washcloths

I was puzzled

Today I lifted the bathroom rug from its folded position

and hastily, a spider ran off it

I used the last of my mousse and froze him against the wall

And I was thinking maybe the spiders don't come up the drain

bypassing four washcloths and two angels

Maybe they come from my bedroom and dive into the tub

And can't get up because it's so slippery

And so the bathtub is probably a trap

So the thing to do is put bathtubs all over the place

Look how much mousse I could save!

*The precious dogs
we were given to love*

Goodnight dearest Zoie

Goodnight

I will miss you when the sun comes up

And the sun goes down

Please come to your park tomorrow

Meet me there at noon

We'll walk quietly together as we always did

Goodnight dearest Zoie

Goodnight

Forever,

Mama

My darling Zoie

I think of you all the time

Dearest friend

I see you dawdling on our lazy walks

And then I see your eyes meeting mine

We are going to visit you in the park

Next Saturday November 13th

Oh Zo you're smiling…yes yes…we're coming

We will be there at noon

My heart, my Zoie girl

Zoie slipped away 3 months ago

And Rock slipped into my heart

He's a very special baby boy

he's gained seven pounds,

it's that old adage...

if you want to win

don't ever look a dog in the eyes

he hides behind my legs when

Dad wants to take him for a walk

Dad is pretty disappointed without a walking partner

Dad says we need a dog shrink

I say maybe Dad shouldn't have walked my baby boy 5 miles

I'm cookin' Rock a bone

One thing I'm sure of

Rock will not go to a Shrink

without me

The heir to Zoie's throne

WHAT TO DO WITH ALL THAT PAIN

Almost everyone said "wait"

When you're past post menopausal you don't wait

for love. My friend Bear and I spent 4 hours

at the Longmont Humane Society

I wanted to take all of them home...

the 115 lb. Shepard...the bronco

Yellow Lab...Max shiny black hair...and then the

kennel keeper admonished me...

"wrong dogs for you lady!"

Four hours later, Bear needed to go back to work

I was still weeping when we left and one of the

administrators invited me to

a support group for loss of pets

I called Mel and he was in so much pain I was scared...Where

was Zoie??

He was now willing to go to Boulder to find a baby

On the way to Boulder we stopped to see the dogs

Bear and I had seen in the a.m.

Mel laughed at the 115 lb. Shepard...asked to walk with

Bo the 7 month old yellow lab...this would be quite a coup

"I'll be able to train him," Mel said

As we both were wildly

pulled across the dirt almost falling down

while the kennel keeper smirked

"Too old for these dogs," Mel said, and we left for Boulder

It was there in two minutes

Mel found him. I was so glad to see Mel smile again

and so not willing to reject anything

we made an instant decision...cancel all other interests

Here was the heir to Zoie's throne...

not a dog people would look at and say

"what a beautiful dog" like they said about Zoie

He was part Corgi

about 10lbs overweight, like me...and probably needed cataract

surgery like me...

He was a gentle dog like Zoie...

a red dog like Zoie...

He needed us like Zoie

We needed him like we needed Zoie...

A sweet dog like our Zoie

Goodnight dearest Zoie

With all my heart forever

If dogs could talk

When we adopted Rock

He couldn't bark—after weeks of coddling and praise a shriek

of a bark was born

This only happened when a person in one of the four

condominiums made a movement

When I had to leave

I left him with my daughter and her family

They had a big dog named Luna

Luna was crazy also

A fenced yard with a glitch

On the other side of the fence live two barking dogs that never

go in their house

Rock loves to run next to the fence and bark his head off

And Luna offers back-up barking

I need to teach them how to talk

I can no longer bear the barking

Has anyone heard of a school that teaches dogs to talk?

Or is there someone out there that needs a barking dog?

Rock and I are bullied by Boo Radley

Boo Radley did not look like a cat afraid

of a dog the other day

He looked more like a lion

He made himself bigger

A technique that I heard of

if confronted by a grizzly bear

He scratched at Rock

My Rock cried out

I screamed at Boo

He confronted me also

I found the courage to grab Boo

and close the sliding glass door

and created a barrier between all of us

I am now the helpless baby sitter

I cannot leave the room

"Mila, please climb over the other baby barrier

and close the bedroom door"

This cat was no dummy

"The door to Mama and Papa's room is closed," Mila said

Boo Radley was still very intimidating

He would not back down

"You know Grandma this is Boo Radley's house"

Mila reminded me as I created a barricade with doll houses

so I wouldn't see the giant Boo looking at me

"Mila, I don't think Rock can sleep over while me and

Grandpa go on vacation"

"Yes," said Mila, "you're right Grandma"

Rock has found his voice

Ever since that night more than 10 years ago

when Day, Russ, Di and I were held up

and they had a gun in Russell's throat and Russell spoke and

saved us

I had the voice of Zoie to tell me something was coming

I liked that

And now dear Rock has found his voice

It is that of a wolf, like Russell's was that night

I like that

I heard that the moon is out with Venus tonight

Rock and I went for our walk today

This boy is so adorable, so irrepressibly lovable

He's a dog

I'm getting used to the idea

This is a right pawed dog

and I'm a left handed person

Finally I have retrained my brain so I can walk with

a right pawed dog

My bossy neighbor screamed

"You shouldn't change,

he has to change"

I never listen to people with their

Out of control discipline ideas

Me and Rock kept walking and laughing

When suddenly

he saw a squirrel

Not a fast New York squirrel

This was

a very slow squirrel

Rock's ears were erect

He looked like a hunter

"Leave it Rock" I said in dog language

He looked at me and listened

We kept walking

The squirrel still was acting pretty dumb

This was not a New York Squirrel

We were now inches away

Rock was really into it

"Squirrel, do you see us" I screamed

"Leave it Rock"

The squirrel finally heard me

"Good boy Rock"

I'm going to get you a big bonie

Rock jumped to the sky

I laughed and said

"Is that O.K. Zoie"

I saw her big doe eyes pretty annoyed

with the whole incident

I love you Zoie

Zoie and Rock and my social life

I had never had a dog like Zoie

She loved to play with other dogs

She lived in their world of a

secret language of dogs

They would put their paws down… rear up

A signal with an eye and away they ran

It's a lot of fun watching dogs play

and you meet a lot of people

The common ground

They love to watch their dogs play also

Zoie had friends

They all came to her 11th birthday party last

Mother's Day. They played, ate their bones

and then they left

Rock does not like to socialize

He tolerates Luna

and endures the kitty Buddy Boy-Girl-Daffodil sniffing him

Rock has brushed off all of Zoie's friends

He is focused

Sure do miss Zoie and her friends

and the games they used to play

Starting classes to teach dogs to talk

Why didn't anyone think of this sooner?

I came out of a store and three huge dogs were

barking in unison

I could tell they were sweet dogs so I moved closer

to their car

Wouldn't you rather talk than bark?

They seemed interested

They all got quiet

I started singing

"The first three letters just happen to be"

I was sure I heard them say A B C

And they stopped barking!

This was going to be easy

I'll make a business plan tomorrow

Can you just imagine a dog coming to the door

to greet you?

And says A B C

Day three of teaching dogs how to talk instead of barking

Dana has agreed to start a singing class for

the "gifted" dogs

I knew this was going to be a "business"

I wonder if she could teach them "My Funny Valentine"

Please join us as we change the world

At the front entrance of the Mountain View Cemeteries

tomorrow

We will be most welcome there

Next year I'm going to advertise on the Super Bowl game

Wow, I just love when the pieces come together

Rock is telling me he needs to go out

It's 10:30

Come on Rock

Hurry

I open the door

And see what I have seen

Thousands of times before

And yet I wanted to yell

"Hi Moon, it's me Lila

You are so full and beautiful

Thanks for coming out tonight"

Thanks Rock for showing me the way.

Rock's on a low-carb diet

He weighed 36 lbs when we got him

He weighs 42 lbs. now

He's a lot like Keanie

A vacuum cleaner for all the food

Will, Mila, Maedee, Julea and Ben

carry or drop, everywhere they go

Well the Vet gave me low-carb food for my Rock

I love him so much

I just won't look in his eyes

While he dances around me

Rock you'll thank me one day

Me the great disciplinarian

Rock, my fella

The ride of life is so fast

I hardly notice time going by

It's almost a year since I lost My Zoie

And I remember when Zoie first came to us

And I watched her happy with a bone

When will she forget her pain?

And in the same year my heart bent for My Zoie girl

I fell in love with Rock, My Fella

My heart bends as his confidence grows

As he takes more and more steps away from me

He has forgotten the pain

And life goes on

And that's a good thing

The seasons that I missed the 50 years I lived in Miami Beach and California

&

My love affair with the moon

A room of one's own

It has been a long time

Though not

Since Dad left

Without any obvious notice

So much time has passed and finally some peace tonight

Debra and David with the three little maziks helping

Moved the earth today to make this room a reality

And here I am

I can feel the peace

Even before everyone went to sleep

I felt the peace return to my heart

Rocky has returned to his spot under the bed

Thank you all for so much for your patience and generosity

Through this very hard time

I will so miss my California family

A real writer

I was always a little jealous of Erma Bombeck

She figured out how to be a real writer

And she made me laugh!

All the things she said were true and funny

It would have been a great idea to have a vacuum in the

Basement and at the end of the day just pulled a string

And all would be beautiful again

It would be wonderful if dinner guests could come over

And the rugs and the couches could be stained

Erma got it right

But she had so much money

Why were her couches and rugs dirty?

And see it is

The empty nest again

How I hate giving up the joy of you all

Now I have a luxurious room and bath—and my dog

And all of you to love eternally

Dearest moon

When I woke this morning you

Were waiting for me

You sat

Curved

So bright

Next to the dark blue sky

I love you dear moon

See

My heart flying up to you

Hello Everybody

Another New Year

The years go by

And you don't notice the strength departing also

I watched six of my beloved grandchildren as they lit the

Shabbos Candles

With their Mamas and Papas last night

I felt the aura of magic that I remember

every time I hear those prayers

I could feel my Grandma Dora

joining them at the table and her joy

Watching her great and great great grandchildren

repeating the prayers that she brought with her from Pachive

No one else can confirm that she was from a town in Russia

called Pachive, but that is what I remember when I was sitting

around a table in her kitchen

in a clean cellar with floors she had optimistically scrubbed

to get ready for the Shabbos

Jack and Lisa drove me home in their van

all of us including Rock tucked neatly in

looking for the full moon

The moon was not listening to us

I couldn't find it until I let Rock out

this morning

And there she was, definitely a lady today

"Hi Moon, missed you last night"

Then I thought of the love at

Debra and David's table last night

I was happy Grandma Dora came back

And Mel was smiling

Valentines for Valentine's Day

Today is Valentine's Day

Some people hate it

But me, I love it!

When I first met my husband I begged for a Valentine

Even before he was really mine

He drew me a Cupid on a napkin

Only we would recognize this as the real beauteous Cupid

That I needed it to be

I think he loves me

I thought this quietly to myself

Not wanting to scare him away

When we got married there was not such hoopla about

Valentine's Day

As there is today

And so he would forever forget the day

And if he did remember to

Buy a card it always said,

"To My Wonderful Wife"

And it was unsigned

When I complained he would ask,

"How many husbands do you have?"

He left after Valentines Day in 2005

After 53 years

There was a Rose and a card addressed

"To Lila…My One and Only Love"

In his stunning calligraphy

Still unsigned

Here's to Valentines on Valentine's Day

Spring you've arrived

Spring you've arrived

The birds are singing

Deb's tulips are breaking through the ground

Know that you will leave again

And it will snow before the lilacs bloom

But for today dance with me

Spring

it is a gloomy-gloomy day

the mystery of spring

such great promise

we wait

yesterday it rained and rained and snowed

today the sun peeked out

I'm sure there are azaleas in Norfolk

gorgeous Matisse colors covering the grounds of California

I can't remember spring in Miami Beach

but I do remember great love and strength and growth

I remember Spring in the Catskills

Oh yes, the best spring until Miami Beach

we wait until tomorrow

Hello, it's Spring

The birds were the first to tell me

The dear, dear, beautiful birds, they've come back

I'm glad to tell them that that awful cat Sam is not

In Boulder this week

Oh how I longed to see spring again

Having spent most of my life in Miami Beach

And Los Angeles where it's always Spring

In Boulder, Colorado it is possible to see and feel

An absolute miracle

The snow it began in September

And it kissed every mountaintop

Then melted away

After a while it had to stay

I know it's coming back again

But the tulips and the birds and the daffodils

Refuse to give up our spring

The snow may fall on our Lilacs

But spring will win

Our trees will be dazzling

And I am still here to see you dear wonderful spring

Snow in May-Never in L.A.

I was driving home last night

It was gray and windy and cold

I saw a tree

Covered with millions of white blossoms

This is like an O'Henry story

Immediately another blooming tree

How could one person possibly glue all those pink blossoms

On those branches

Snow began to fall

Oh winter, I hope you don't hurt the blossoms

People that have lived here for a while say

"This is spring in Boulder"

I can't believe it… snow in May?

Never in L.A.

The Solstice

When I was growing up during the depression

The Solstice was never referenced in my life

"My Mother told me I was born on the

longest day of the year"

My husband would remind me each year

With such incredible tenderness

In his eyes

Our son Jack was born on that day of days

My dear friend Toby's birthday was the Winter Solstice

The shortest day of the year

Did everyone always know of the Solstice?

I didn't until Jack told me!

And then Toby left on the longest day of the year

Happy Birthday dear Toby

Yesterday we turned the clocks back

Yesterday we turned the clocks back

Thereby gaining an hour

I awoke at 6

It was really 5

But I thought it was 7

So I ate breakfast

By the time it was 9:30

I was ready for lunch because

It was 4 and 1/2 hours since

I had breakfast

By 4 p.m. I still had gained only

One hour

And 5 pounds

Just turned out the light

And there is that full moon again

Big, white

So bright

Thanks for saying hi

I love you moon

You are so handsome

Goodnight

Rosh Hashanah with my Grandma Dora

Rosh Hashanah was serious business for us

My three brothers, my sister and me

When we were young

Saturday was big, but the Jewish Holidays

Were bigger

We all got dressed in winter clothes and they were always

The hottest days of the year

We didn't have a car so the "no driving" rule

didn't effect us at all

I remember there was no writing, no scissors, no cooking

My Grandfather spent his days at the shul dovening

There was no school for two days

These two days and three others were called

Jewish Holidays

Wherever you went everyone said "Happy New Year"

It was very strange because

It was always very sad for me

Sukkot

Yesterday was an exciting holiday

First a full moon arrived

the biggest moon that you ever did see

to announce it

And then there was the Trank-Greene's sukkah

that Papa Jack had built

And the children and Deb and Lisa (the Mamas)

were happily making wreaths and covering the beautiful

sukkah with leaves

And dried flowers and pinecones hung

with mint dental floss

that Lisa supplied

Jack was doing last minute touches of enclosing the sukkah

with fabric to shelter us from

the winds that had suddenly become cold

We sat on chairs at a table

and then magically we all were served a delicious hot

vegetable soup that Deb had made

Did I mention the love that was in that backyard?

There is a full moon tonight

Though I wasn't expecting it until tomorrow

I can see it clearly as the branches sway on the Aspen tree

It's always a surprise

Never a matter of fact

There is a full moon again tonight

It was as natural as the laughing children running with the adorable puppy Milo

And there were Mila, Will, Ben, Maedee, Julea and Meggie on the swings

Or was it Jack, Dana, Russ, Deb and Bob?

For a moment it was

What a happy time

Jack brought a picture of Mel laughing so merrily

And he sat at the table with us loving his family

As always

This is a very different fall

I've heard that every sunset is different

and so I am not surprised

This is a very different fall

There are falls that arrive with harsh winds and blow so many

leaves away

Never giving them a chance to whisper goodbye

This fall is slow and gentle and the paintbrush of color on

every leaf tells a story

This fall isn't rushing

It's prancing and dancing and saying,

"Look at me, I love you."

And I so want to kiss them back

Oh fall, you are the most beautiful of all

Thanks for letting me see you again in your amazing

splendor

It's Sunday, it's Halloween

8:25 A.M.

My husband says

"Did you change the clocks?"

It looks like 8:24 A.M.

I immediately changed the main clock

To 9:24

And thought the only thing that gets this right

is the cell phone

I looked at my cell phone and it says 7:34

For a minute I'm all mixed up

And then I get it

"Fall Back"

I go back to the main clock

And change it from 9:24 to 7:24

Thereby gaining 2 hours in 2 minutes

Trick or Treat?

Yesterday the winds arrived

They were more brutal than before

And then Russ reminded me

Of Frost saying in another millennium

"nothing gold can stay"

I'm trying to hold on to the beauty of yesterday

And then Russ said quoting Williams

"We were all beautiful once"

The aspen leaves we glued on paper for our

Thanksgiving placemats were no longer glowing

"What about this?" Deb asked me

Apparently annoyed at the endless clutter

"Is it no longer beautiful?" I asked as it

quickly landed in the trash

I went to my car and millions of leaves were under my shoes

I will never forget how beautiful fall was yesterday as

The sun made everything a gold that looked like it would stay

forever

Another round of beauty

There are chrysanthemums and marigolds bursting out of

the ground

This is an extra season

We've gotten a beautiful gift

Come dance with us they are saying

The Russian Sage fragrance is delicious

There are berries all over the place

They are red and announcing that more are coming

Laugh with us

There's an extra season to remember before

the blustery days blow in

In 2007, another round of beauty

The many seasons of the fall

In October, especially in Boulder, Colorado

Because we are so close to the sun

There is the first act of fall

One of ravishing color

And when the skies turn gray

That is the second act of fall

For without the sun the beauty of the colors disappear

And I am saddened

The third act of fall is when the sun comes back and it is beautiful again

Only now the colors are monochromatic. It all goes together like a beach

Blue skies, sandy colored almost barren trees

And then as the grand finale to fall

Snow comes flying in and covers everything

With a white magic

And the sun keeps shining in Colorado

**Is it possible that enough has been said
about the colors of fall?**

No oh no

Every time I see a new burst of color

I think I'm in Africa

There is nothing as beautiful as the fall

Especially this fall

In Colorado

All of a sudden on a desolate piece of road

There is a great big giant glorious yellow tree

You are breathtaking

I need to stop

I would love to hug you

And down the road there are reds and browns

and orange trees

all with a breeze floating over them

Oh thank you fall for coming again while I'm still here

A fifth season – charting the slow departure of summer

And I was thinking it's another season

There is a fifth season and it is where the colors of

Thanksgiving came from. They are staying –

Mums and Zinnias all Thanksgiving flowers

I saw a tree doing pirouettes yesterday

Round and round

It was like a movie. The leaves were dancing and hundreds of

them were falling –

Beautiful small yellow leaves

Doing a ballet and bowing as

they fell on the leaves that had danced their way

down first –

The extra season that would not leave without a

well-deserved "encore"

I remember the spring when I was so glad to see your green

leaves struggling to come out from under the snow when I lost

Mel

I think you are happiest now for you know you are so

magnificent, brilliant, beauteous and joyful

Be gentle cold winds on these beautiful trees

I love them so

Winter for an old California princess

I get in my car

It is 10 degrees outside

I can't see how to get the car in the way of the Dracula sun

I wait

Listen to "NPR"

Growl at Bush and Cheney

There is still ice blocking my view

I wait

I am an old lady

I wait some more

I have great expectations

David returns from dropping Will off at school

He immediately sees my plight and slowly and laboriously he scrapes the ice

From even the sides of the car

Sometimes it's fun to be an old lady

2007

Right?

Last year I had an accident driving on an icy freeway

My car just changed lanes by itself

It was an out of body experience

The car corrected itself and came back to the lane it had left

And was promptly rear-ended

This was not a dream

It reminded me of Raymond Carver's line

"It's all gravy and don't forget it"

I'm so grateful for you all in my life

Happy Holidays

And here's to 2007…right?

My beloved husband Mel

When Mel and I were very young

We worked at Grossinger's

In the Catskill Mountains

Once Eddie Fisher and

Debbie Reynolds visited

My Mel was taking a picture with

Debbie Reynolds

The very young version, sitting on his lap

I was so, so jealous

And while this was happening Elizabeth Taylor walked away

with Eddie Fisher

When Lila met Mel in 1954 he was a band singer

At the Grossinger Hotel in the Catskill Mountains
Her life prior to meeting Mel was very, very sad and
She became totally absorbed in musical comedy
She was obsessed with Oklahoma, Carousel, Pajama Game
And Cole Porter's Can Can
She really didn't know she couldn't sing
A happy-go-lucky spirit she memorized all the lyrics
From the day they met he would sing all day, and her role was
to coach him on the lyrics
When they married, the singing would continue
day and night
He was obsessed with singing

And in the eight years the five babies came
the singing never stopped
As the babies grew they all began playing guitar and piano
And Mel kept singing and singing and singing
We would host parties so that we could have an audience
The house was filled with music
And their music rose above the neighborhood

Lila kept thinking this was the Von Trapp family

Everyone hated that idea and they

All pursued their music in their own way

They all are so talented and music indeed became

their life also

It was a house filled with artists

And it all seemed so natural

We were a real show business family with all the magic

I had dreamed of

The hard part is that woman's liberation popped up

in the middle of all this

And my role was that I knew nothing

There were definitely musical genes

on my side of the family also

My mother's sister Viola singing in Radio City Hall

And my father's brother Uncle Mike

who played the piano in spite of

a world of poverty, depression and anger

Mel would wake up and before getting dressed

standing in his jockey shorts

he would begin to sing

Sometimes he wasn't singing, he was just playing back his
recordings and listening to them over and over
Sometimes I would think the recordings were live
and I would be surprised as I looked in the room
and the music continued while he listened and showered
It was as if he was going for the discovery of penicillin
He was so dedicated
"Mel, enough" I would say
"No, no I must find the right way" he insisted
The kids naturally all became a part of this "quest"
He would ask anyone of us who was around
"Come listen, which way do you like it?
Or do you like it this way?"
By this time I was ready to kill him
This could not be my real life
His clothes were hung in a "stellar" fashion
And his shoes stored neatly with shoetrees within each one
There was not a night that he would go to bed
with his clothes not put away
When he went to a gig
he carefully ironed his tux and his shirts

and would carry them to the gig

and whatever it took

he would find a place to change

so that not a wrinkle would set upon him

When he went out to sing he was Pavarotti

And he was going to Carnegie Hall

When we lost our hero we all stood looking at his wardrobe

What could be done with it?

While I was still thinking that he wasn't going to record again

my daughters Dana and Debra grabbed his two tuxedoes

and decided there had to be a show

"SONG'S MY FATHER SANG"

And so on November 5th, Saturday at 7PM in the year 2005

Mel Greene's five magnificent children

that all inherited his voice and dedication

will sing to honor their Dad

My husband

My Pavarotti

Dad

I was chasing Dad all over the planet for three years

And then at the New York Public Library he said,

"O.K., I'll marry you"

One of the happiest days of my life

We both worked in New York City then

It was after he left Grossinger's for a record deal

and me – devastated that I had lost him forever

The record deal never worked out

I was working at a photography studio

and he at a men's haberdashery on Fifth Avenue

We started going out again

Every night after work we would meet at Schrafts

It was the kind of place that served sandwiches

with the crusts cut off

I could not bear to separate from him

His beautiful face and hands

Letters to my husbands

On our 10th anniversary

I gave my husband a medal

For meritorious service

I adored him

And he adored me

The following year I got him a Superman Pin

I couldn't have loved him more

He would take me to Mike Gordon's for seafood dinners

We had friends

We were so happy

We adored our five children

and we remained madly in love

I actually created the $10\frac{1}{2}$ pin to honor him

and then he left Sammy Davis Jr. and

nothing ever again

would be the same

Letters to my husbands

I miss one of my husbands

The endearing one

that would make me dinner

make me tea

Cover me with a blanket

Tell me I was more beautiful than when

we fell in love 53 years ago

I felt pain in the supermarket the other day

when a woman said to the clerk

"No thank you, I'm waiting for my husband!"

My good husband has gone away

And I am left without my dearest friend

Letters to my husbands

It is almost a month since

my son Jack and I watched in disbelief and horror

my good husband's seizure

before the crew of many

ambulance, fire department, paramedics

crowded into the room

where he lay upon the bed

with Jack kissing his forehead

and assuring him that help was indeed with us

This man who called me sweetheart

I had never seen him like this before

It was over then

But we were in too much shock to know it

This crew of people had come so many times before

And my good husband would not succumb

It is almost a month

as I walk around aimlessly

without anyone to call me sweetheart

Again

Letters to my husbands

Of course I'm going to make the Matzo Ball Soup

for Passover

The best in the world

Me, I always got all the credit

Carrots, onions, leek, parsley, parsnip, dill

and chicken

Oh man, where is my prep person?

Only one person who would neatly clean and chop

each vegetable in a separate bowl

(Why was that necessary?)

Come back and I won't complain

I will even call it Mel's Soup

Oh man, where is my prep person?

Letters to my husbands

It is a month since you slipped away from me

And I really miss you

I don't think your ashes can hear me

You are in my dreams

They are dreamy dreams

I need to find you

Show me the way

I really miss you

Today is May 13th

And it's Friday

My broken heart is easing up on me

I miss you my beloved husband

I wished I had smiled at you more

Hugged you more

I so hope you know that I loved you so

from the first moment I saw your face

on stage in the Terrace Room at Grossinger's in 1954

I fell madly in love with you

My darling Mel

I miss you so

Hello my Mel

It is May 20th, almost 2 months since you

left without a word

I am getting ready to go to see our children in L.A.

I miss your "good morning sweetheart"

even your grumpy morning habits

and questions

Who will carry my luggage down the steps?

and help get Rock and his food in the car?

Should I take your ashes part way to The Joshua Tree?

Yesterday I did not move all day

Will you come with me anyway?

I'll buy you gum

And the New York Times

And yes, please help me down the steps with this luggage

I love you,

Lila

Letters to my husbands

Month 2

I went back to our apartment today

You, of course, were not there

Someone came to the door

and Rock's bark was enough for the person

to say to me, "you can come out"

I was there to meet the carpet measuring person

I wondered how he could do that if I came out

"Your name please?"

"I'm John, here to deliver your husband's death certificates"

"Here's the invoice"

"Thank you," I said

I went to the closet and smelled your suits

I closed my eyes and wedged my way in

"It's not the pale moon that excites me

that thrills and delights me, oh no –

It's just the nearness of you"

Letters to my husbands

I always loved to dance with him

It was beautiful dancing

I loved the love-songs

especially "The Nearness of You"

I loved the nearness of him

When he would leave Grossinger's

the hotel where we worked

I would stay in his room and hug his clothes

We started going to Broadway shows together

The Pajama Game, Can Can, Kismet

We were falling madly in love

And soon we would have our great adventure

and stay together overnight at the Taft Hotel in NYC

This was only a few years before the movie *The Graduate*

We were in the same elevator going "UP"

Mel wore a hat (as he usually did)

And was pretending to read a newspaper

He looked right out of a Perry Mason movie

It's so sweet because in 1954 this was very unique behavior

Everything was wrong that night at the Taft Hotel

But how I wish we could be there tonight

Dancing to "The Nearness of You"

Two sad months

And 9 months of growth

Our Meggie trying to stand

My Mellie comforting me

And life goes on

And that's a good thing

The birthday - June 21, 1957

My first baby was due on June 12th

and it's pretty hot in Miami Beach in June

I am a very impatient person

I won't even wait for a cake to cool

before I ice it

Each extra day – grueling

Then the prize –

The scream

"A boy on my birthday!!"

When our first prize was one year old

I needed a brilliant thought to have written

on this birthday cake

"Happy Birthday to Jackie and His Daddy"

And again on June 21, 2005

June 21, 2005

I didn't meet him in 1954

It was 1953

There was nothing before him

And everything with him

And now he is

playing with his brother

talking to his Mother

helping out Rosie Philo

He was always talking

But never about this

I can sleep if he's calm

It would be good if this were true

If you talk to him again

Please say

"Wait for me

I'm here for you"

My beloved

Can you really reach your beloved after he's left the planet

as we know it?

Yesterday Dana and Russ did just that

They were reunited with their Dad after a three-month absence

His mother and my mother and his brother found him

He was happy

Vivacious

And waiting for his beloved family to find him

He knew we were listening to Al Green that day

He's sticking around for a while

I'm glad

There's so much to say

I love you

So glad you get to play with your brother

A red plaid bathing suit for Mel

Happy Birthday my love

I so wish you were here

and I wouldn't be alone

I was always with you

and never thought it could end

Flighty old woman

Took it all for granted

I hope you're in my dream tonight

and it is sweet and beautiful

The way it was

The way it was

when we were very young

And the first of a lifetime of birthdays

I gave you a red plaid bathing suit

June 26th, 2005

Today is the anniversary

Of when you went away

The tears come less often now

I remember when it was totally raw

And if someone said "hi"

I would cry and tell them

Please not to speak of you

Sometimes I call your name

and I think

This is a good thing

I love you still

Shall we have cake?

There are 365 days in a year

I decide to check messages

on our answering machine

There are many shocked people leaving messages

The operator says

"This message has been saved for 100 days

the maximum time allowed!"

"Lila this is Barbara"

"Lila this is Paul"

"Lila this is Mim"

"I'm so sorry to hear the devastating news"

I hit #5 which will tell me the date of these calls

Monday, March 27th

There are 365 days in a year

You have been gone 101 days

And I really miss you

My darling husband, August 14th, 2005

We often joked about either one of us

rushing off to find a new boyfriend or girlfriend

when one of us would be gone

We both said that would never happen

And I'm so glad I still feel that way

Truly

You are my one and only love,

Li

It is Sunday in the middle of August 2005

My dear sweet husband,

An armoire that has traveled with our family

for more than 30 years has just arrived

from Russ, Di, and Georgia's house

I look in its mirror and see Georgia dressed

in costumes for many Halloweens

I also see her twirling around in a ballerina costume

and I'm looking closer

There are kisses all over the mirror

just about Georgia's height

Everything that goes around

comes around again

with kisses

Life is indeed a mirror

Letters to my husbands - September 2005

Last night I dreamed about you

We were fighting

I was competing with you

No, no, I said, not again

I was going to support you

and get you directions to your singing gig

I kept asking for the spelling of the street

I was writing it down

Finally, really annoyed, she hung up

Suddenly we were in what could have been Loehmann's

My precious husband

In the Broadway show about baseball

one of the most wonderful songs was

"A man doesn't know what he has until he loses it"

And now I know I miss you so

Thank you for taking such good care of me

Thanks for emptying the dishwasher and loading it also

Thanks for taking all those hateful jobs

to take care of us

You were so stoic

I can no longer stay here without you

I smell your hair

Your beautiful hair

I remember so many times when you told me

you dreamed of me

And now I dream of you

You are my one and only love

How lucky we were

we found each other

and made this beautiful family together

Talented, charming,

kind

They are taking such good care of me

They said you told them to

Thank you, please follow me to Venice

I'll sit on the beach and watch you walk

My precious husband, let's go back to the beach

I'm taking you with me on the plane

I'm so glad I married you

Love,

Li

Finally a sweet, sweet dream

I dreamed about my husband last night

And the part that woke me up

was him saying,

"You're flirting with me"

And I was laughing

And he kept saying it

"You're flirting with me"

And I kept laughing

My darling husband

Miss you in a way that is indescribable

Only retrievable

In an old love song

like

"Night and Day"

That makes me cry

like it did when we broke up

oh so many times before

"Day and Night

under the heart of me."

Miss you in a way that is indescribable

And the tears keep running down my face

Letters to my husbands

I am in Deb and David's guest room

Although they graciously call it: Grandma's room

I am watching a tree as its leaves bloom

even as it snows upon them

It is a very tedious process

and hardly resembles what will become

willowy Aspen leaves

Soon it will be warm and we will forget the icy streets

the barren trees

I will long for your warm embrace

Hard to be alone and have no one to turn to

And that is why I can't stay here alone

When my husband was here

he would walk in and turn on the lights

I liked the maleness of things like that

"Why hadn't I left a light on?" I thought

as I felt the extra rug

stopping me under my feet

"Be slow," I said to myself

But I didn't hear

The kitchen lights were on and compulsively

I went to see if there were any emails

I walked into the computer room

forgetting I had left the luggage on the floor

I tripped, banged my head on the metal bed frame

I was lucky I could feel the spirits in the room

They were protecting me

I went to the freezer

Said hi to Maedee and Julea's placentas

Got what was left of Mel's spelt bread

Sat down with the bread on the lump on my head

And thought, I'm glad my kids like me

Over again

If I had my life to live over again

I would definitely not be a feminist

I would not do comedy based upon my husband

I would instead be the wife

I was expected to be in 1956

I do not know why I was part of this movement

I just loved the love songs

And him singing to me

Perhaps he'll come by and he'll sing

"If I Loved You" or "Someday she'll come along"

And we will kiss and laugh again

Do you think this could happen?

"Yes it can happen to you if you're young at heart"

I will wait for this enchanted time to come again

I contacted a medium

She had spoken to Mel before on my behalf

He was very happy and sent so much love to me

I felt good

That was months ago and I asked her to

speak with him for me again

She asked me if I had any questions for him

Yes, I wanted him to stay longer in my dreams

and hug me longer and tighter

He answered me last Friday

He was very happy "on the other side"

But his angels were very worried

about my obsessive interest in him

Why wasn't I more involved over here?

He said that he would always love me,

but I should look for a real person on "this side"

What?

Would he really say that?

Of course he was always saying the wrong thing

and boy was I mad

I responded to the medium and I said "what a vacancy"

"Yes I can imagine, but did you get anything out of it?"

"Nothing."

I erased the whole message

What happened?

Who decides if you are allowed to live

with the memories of love?

You're not allowed to say "I miss him"

Who makes the rules?

You spend your whole life with one person

And when I speak of him my brother-in-law

and others change the subject

Move on, they insist

Where am I going?

I just packed up all his pictures and Zoie's

All his clothes and ties and Zoie's collar and ID

I'm taking them all out again

I'll do what I want

You better come with Zoie in my dream tonight

And you better hold me tight

I miss my husband

His name is Mel

And I miss my dog

Her name is Zoie

I hope they're listening to me

I dreamed about my husband last night

I was so glad to see you!

I put my arms around you

And you lightly returned the hug

Look I have corned beef for sandwiches

"No, no" he said

"I'm going to have a bagel

Do you want a bagel?"

And then you were gone

And I woke up thinking that I couldn't hug you anymore

But I was so glad you are in my dreams

See you later my love

We still loved each other

There was hardly any touching

So missed the touching

What was left of a beautiful love?

He had become so remote

So distant

I had lost him

He only wanted to sit in his room

and listen to recordings of himself

Or make new recordings

There was the "News Hour"

There was "Meet the Press"

And there was "60 Minutes"

None of these could be missed

There was the morning greeting:

"Good morning sweetheart"

The report on how badly the night had gone

And then the offer to make me oatmeal

And then at least an hour with the empty Daily Camera

There were no goals

Only perhaps a lab test to complete

a trip to the gym to walk and stretch

There were no other occasions to remember

except his brothers' and CeCe's birthdays

If I complained he quickly asked to make me tea

vacuum the rug

That was all that was left

And I really love him

And I really miss him

And I wish I could kiss him again

on his sweet cool lips

You

I miss you so much right now

My dearest

My love

My best friend

You

Today I was thinking about things I had left in the car

I'm too tired to go out to get them

You would always go and get them for me

You

For more than 50 years you would do things for me

I wish you would come back

And I could say "thank you"

You, you, you

It's November 17th

We did the show 2 weeks ago

I watched in awe

Dad stood next to me

And we looked in each other's eyes

the way people do

after spending their lives together

And we saw our golden children on the stage

Our dearest children

All so brilliant, so sensitive, and so smart

It was a show for Dad

and he said

"Li, we did it!"

I nodded and smiled

We were both so proud

As the next generation came to the stage

and we all took a bow

How much you all loved your Dad and Grandpa

You are such wonderful kids

Thank you

You did good!

Love, marriage, guilt and grief

We were together for 53 years

I was a very young and a very old 23

Women knew nothing according to men in those days

and with a father like mine

going to college was only for boys

Girls were expected to find a husband

I always knew I was a writer…always

I registered at NYU for classes in literature

I had absolutely no support

I am now astounded at how I got to Washington Square

and back to Jamaica

alone on the subway and buses

I used to go to Chock Full of Nuts before class

They served great coffee

and date and nut bread sandwiches with cream cheese

And divine hotdogs

it was very unique

Only African Americans worked there

and I think I wondered why

there were no dishes

Everything was served

on a kind of paper you get in a bakery

And somehow I got from there to a classroom

and home again

I had a job, an abusive father and stepmother

I saw a lot of movies and made up my life based on that

Through some divine intervention

My sister helped me get a job at the fabulous

Grossinger Hotel in the Catskill Mountains

The staff lived and played there

And then the happiest day of my life, a year later

there he was

I loved him from that first moment

and then forever

We would make each other crazy after twenty years

There was no money and no material possessions

We had five gorgeous very talented dear children

But the disappointment of the loss of status overtook us

and we took it out on each other

So many bridges were built

So painful

We had lost touch with the laughter

and the knowledge that together we had produced

our five extraordinary children

Since my Mel passed almost 2 years ago

I so wanted to rerun everything

I'm so sad that I was so mad

How stupid…why couldn't my head hear my heart

I so want to tell people to not punish their beloved

Not for a moment

I am filled with grief and guilt

I am still in love with my husband

Such a nice thing being married

I love you madly Mel and I'm so sorry

I didn't tell you so every moment

And the pain will not go away

I miss you so much

Thank you for being my best friend forever

and my one and only love

Thank you for that singing sperm

You will be here forever

I love you

And I still remember our first Valentine's Day

And your drawing on the Grossinger cocktail napkin

And our many, many times at the Rainbow Room

in Rockefeller Center

You the most endearing human on the planet

I love you forever,

Lila

Grief three years later

When you left I couldn't even speak of you without crying

I did not want to talk to anyone

only our children

and those who truly loved us

And now, though three years have almost passed

I always wake up in the morning

expecting to see you

We are all different with how we want to spend the time

that is still to come

after the "love of our lives" dies

I don't think anyone knows how this feels

until it happens to

you

Notes

www.pages-lilagreene.com